The Principles and Practices of *Universal* Enhancement

The Principles and Practices of *Universal* Enhancement

Volume Three:
Obstacles to Opportunities

by Thomas E. Pomeranz, Ed.D.

Edited by Virginia Vath

Foreword by Peggy Gould

High Tide Press
Homewood, Illinois

A HIGH TIDE BOOK
Published by High Tide Press Inc.
3650 West 183rd Street, Homewood, Illinois 60430
www.hightidepress.com / toll-free: 1-800-698-3979

Pomeranz, Thomas E. The principles and practices of Universal
Enhancement / by Thomas E. Pomeranz, Ed.D.
Volume 3. First ed.

ISBN 1-892696-17-7

Edited by Virginia Vath
Cover illustration by Barton Stabler
Cover and book design by Diane J. Bell

Printed in the United States of America

First Edition

Printed on acid-free paper. ∞

To my wife, Diane–my partner, inspiration and chief of the UE Police.

Table of Contents

Foreword

My family and I are segment hikers on the Appalachian Trail. Shortly after initiating this venture, I attended a training session led by Dr. Tom Pomeranz focusing on Universal Enhancement.

Surprisingly, he used a term I had only seen associated with the Trail, the use of "stiles" to cross over barriers and move forward. This intrigued me because that is precisely what occurs during a hike. When facing a barrier such as a farmer's stonewall, a barbed wire fence, a creek that limits passage, or a great divide between two mountain shelves, you use a stile to get across and move forward on the path.

The wonderful aspect of a stile is that it enables you to keep moving ahead on your journey. If you have ever hiked, you know that reaching the top of a mountain is only achieved through diligence and determination. But once there, you enjoy great vistas and visions that truly define quality of life. You experience the pleasure of being a part of something bigger than you are. You reach a vantage point from which you can see far distances.

Dr. Pomeranz challenges us to offer support stiles to people with developmental disabilities. A stile is really a covenant of trust, a belief that it will afford safe passage. In our field, we offer stiles enabling and supporting people to endure struggle and find within themselves assurance to advance despite barriers.

Reaching the top of the mountain always brings with it a sense of personal satisfaction. It also provides a sense of immense personal pride.

The theories and maxims offered through Universal Enhancement foster personal achievement. They are methodologies, techniques to support people with developmental disabilities as they move along their life's path. Universal Enhancement provides ideas and is a compass that guides, even on those days when landmarks are few.

Margaret J. (Peggy) Gould
The VISIONS Center for Creative Management
P.O. Box 124
Katonah, New York 10536

Introduction

Universal Enhancement is not a new invention; it is, rather, a discovery. It is a key to unlock and open the closed doors that have served as barriers to countless persons who have been shut out of the world most individuals take for granted. It is the key to a world in which all people are allowed to have a life. It is a magic key in that its use requires not only using the right words, but also the motivation to do things differently. This book can be used as a key, but it is only a tool. You will have to bring your own resources to bear, as you use this tool to help people unlock new opportunities for themselves and their communities.

The notion that some people have been "cast out" from the main-

stream of society will be used as the central metaphor. They are Outsiders. The primary examples of the phenomenon of being cast out are those persons who, because of diminished cognitive and adaptive abilities, are considered to have mental retardation or intellectual disabilities.

Universal Enhancement is "universal" because it applies equally to all conditions that have been used as the basis for excluding people from full participation in their own lives. The tools of Universal Enhancement are applicable to all of us, regardless of ability or disability, as we seek to "enhance" the quality of our lives. "Having a life" is a challenge we all face in some form. We all have our demons.

One reason intellectual disabilities is used as the primary exemplar is that the provision of services and supports for people with intellectual disabilities is the field in which I have had the most experience. Unfortunately, the other reason people with intellectual disabilities can serve as examples is that, for the most part, their lives have been stolen from them by the combined forces of ignorance, prejudice and fear.

Someone who works or lives with people who have mental illness, however, would see the opportunities of Universal Enhancement through the lens of that experience. The same holds true for people more familiar with the isolating and deprecating effects of being elderly or having no parents or being an unwed mother. The principles hold true, regardless of the exemplar. As you read through the book, you can mentally substitute the life circumstances with which you are most familiar or concerned (perhaps a challenge you yourself experience) for the one used as an example.

The main narrative of this book, the text of each of the chapters, can be read straight through. It provides all the history, principles and strategies you need for understanding Universal Enhancement. Scattered throughout this narrative are the following sub-sections that can be read or skipped, according to your particular need and interest:

Tales

Tales are illustrative stories, poems and collective conversation culled from the author's 30-plus years of clinical and administrative experience. These stories demonstrate the principles of Universal Enhancement and present concrete visions of how those principles change peoples' lives.

Toolboxes

Toolbox sections are practical techniques and procedures you can use as you implement the principles of Universal Enhancement. They will demonstrate innovative and effective ways of behaving. The checklist and program suggestions on Toolbox pages may be used in your work or efforts to assist others in enhancing the quality of their life.

Maxims

Maxims are short, succinct phrases that encapsulate the tools and approaches of Universal Enhancement. They will form the core of this new approach and will prompt and inspire your new behavior. If your friends, neighbors and coworkers learn the Maxims, you will share a new vocabulary, a short-hand communication device you can use to remind each other of what you are trying to do and where you are trying to go. The author claims no exclusive rights to the ideas contained in this book, because they are ideas found lying about in everyone's lives. They have been gathered and given form, but they came from everyone and thus belong to everyone. They are truly universal.

It is my hope that as you read what is compiled here, you will experience the same kind of "Aha!" feeling I have had as my new perceptions took shape. You might find yourself thinking, "These ideas are so simple; why didn't we think of and use them much earlier?"

The answer lies in our deeply rooted perception of people we see as being radically different from ourselves. This ability to see some groups of people as wholly "other" than ourselves has, historically, allowed us to act in ways we may later find incomprehensible.

Upon touring the Holocaust Museum in Washington, D.C., a young man asked his father, "How could we have done these things to them?" And the father answered, "The first step was using the word 'them.' After that the rest was easy."

This book is the result of many thousands of hours spent working in the field of services for people with disabilities. I must express my deep appreciation to countless teachers, coworkers, and friends, as well as to the people I have served and supported who have helped shape the principles of Universal Enhancement. I hope this book will bring us all more such relationships, more opportunities to learn, to exchange ideas, and to affect the lives of people.

The Principles and Practices of *Universal* Enhancement

1

Supported Routines

Volume Two, *Challenging the Gatekeepers*, reviewed the premise that the Habilitation Model of service provision pursues habilitation as a goal, with movement to a less restrictive environment as the *earned* result. The principles of Universal Enhancement put a new twist on that equation.

The habilitation process provides opportunities for learning. It provides the means for individuals to be enabled to grow, develop and become more independent despite their Outsider status. But habilitation is a result, not a goal. Habilitation results from being an active participant in life. Being afforded an opportunity to participate in all of one's daily routines with necessary supports assures a high level of engagement. And a level of engagement requires interaction with the materials of life, what is called media.

MAXIM: *Habilitation is not a goal; it is a result.*

This sounds like a rather complex process, but it's really just a compact formulation of the way we all acquire new abilities. We learn new skills by being engaged with the objects that we encounter in our life activities. That's what media is; it is *stuff*–things, objects, people, all the thousands of items that surround and enrich our lives.

Think back to your childhood. How did you learn to vacuum the floor? Did someone put you on a floor vacuuming program? Not likely;

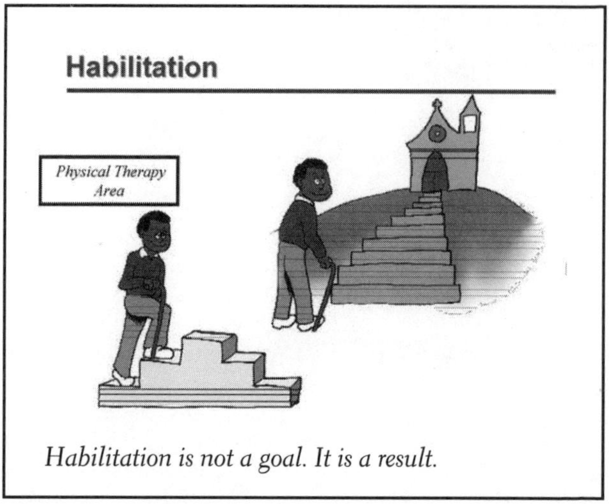

you probably started interacting with the vacuum cleaner (media) by watching Mom or Dad use it. You may have touched it while it was standing there in the middle of the living room. If you saw someone plug it in or turn it on, you may have tried to do it yourself. If there had been no vacuum cleaners in your environment, you would have had no way of learning how to operate one.

The acquisition of language is another good example of how we

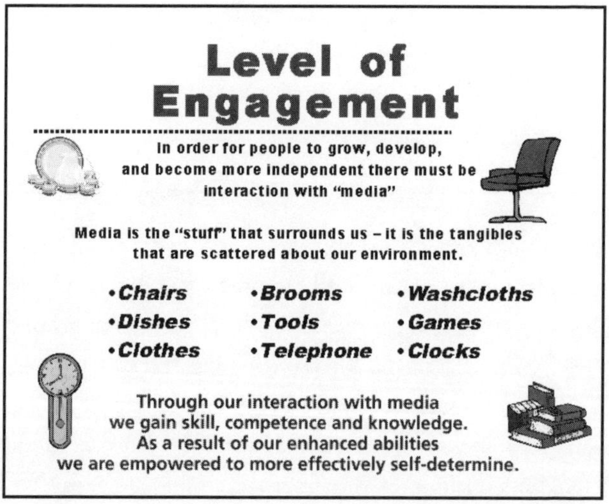

learn new skills through supported routines. Children are seldom taught to talk through some kind of formal instructional system. Instead, they are surrounded by language–spoken, written, gestured, and sung. They are engaged with it and immersed in it all day long. Children absorb language by interacting with it.

In environments with institutional characteristics, the media is scarce, restricted, or contrived. Most of the *stuff* of everyday life is not available for engagement by the people who live there. It is, instead, seen as owned by or under the control of various staff who provide assorted services. The vacuum cleaners are locked up for the sole use of the staff (a use which often occurs after everyone who lives there is in bed or leaves the home for their day program). The food preparation items are in the kitchen that is operated by the staff. The washers and dryers are behind closed, locked doors, operated by staff. Maintenance personnel bring the tools to the job. They change the light bulbs and unstop the toilets.

Lest this description seem limited to the environment of the large, state-operated facility, let's look at a few limitations that occur even in community-based residences. The dining room table has no napkin holder, because Terry eats any paper products she can get her hands

Markers

The Following are examples of "markers" – when present , they provide for a strong indication that the UE Standard is met – this is the type of place I would like to live

- Magazines or books with color photos of interest, in a magazine rack next to the toilet
- A cookie or candy jar filled with tempting items – always accessible
- Adaptive devices in abundance – long handled feather dusters, wash mitts, jelly bean switches, pump coffee pots, comprehensive home chore list – faithfully followed
- Women wearing make-up daily – perhaps a purple stripe in their hair
- Possession and use of sun glasses, rain coats and umbrellas
- Alarm clocks on all night stands – routinely used
- All individuals possess and carry bill-folds – "they do not leave home without them"
- Residents of the home welcome guests and offer them a beverage

on. The TV set is locked up, because Dwayne is fascinated with electronics and takes things apart. The front door is locked so that Melissa won't suddenly run out into the street. Even in small congregate residential or sheltered employment settings, there is often minimal accessibility to the media–the *stuff*, of everyday life that is so necessary for full participation and learning.

MAXIM: *The individual with the most challenging behavior determines the least restrictive environment.*

In lieu of the usual serendipitous access to common media, sometimes special training areas are established. These program rooms, or activities of daily living rooms, are simulation areas in which "clients" can interact with media while they do their scheduled training programs. The vacuum cleaner may be gotten out of the storage closet, if a person has a vacuuming goal on his Individual Habilitation Plan (IHP). Someone may be presented with items of differing texture in the sensory integration rooms. People get together to practice social interaction skills in the social skills training area that looks like a normal living room but is actually in another building from the one in

which individuals live. Training is contrived in such situations, and learning does not come about in the way most of us have naturally experienced it, through our daily interaction with a lot of *stuff*.

Typical institutional settings provide by their very nature (see Volume One, *It Matters How We Say It*, Chapter 1) minimal opportunities to interact with media. There is not much *stuff* available, and the items that are present are usually only accessible at appointed times and with designated supervision.

Supported Routines

As a result of people not being active participants in their daily routines, some very unpleasant things occur. Where there is little to do, little that needs to be done, and not much *stuff* with which to do it, people will more often than not use their creativity to devise nonproductive and/or destructive activities. A human being must always exhibit some kind of behavior; he or she must be doing something, regardless of how sparse the environment. We should not be surprised, therefore, when a man who lives in a barren, institutional environment steals a handful of rice from the plate of a man seated nearby at the Chinese restaurant. Who can blame the woman with no control over most facets of her life for kicking us in the shins? Where there are minimal opportunities, decreased choices, and lack of control in one's environment, alternative behaviors are more likely to develop. Where there are limited opportunities to be an active participant in one's daily routines, it is likely there will be an increase in:

1. Stereotypical behavior. This is the sort of purposeless, repetitive motion that is so striking to the first-time visitor to any institutional setting. People rock, moan, or wave their hands in front of their eyes like some endless, predictable, idiosyncratic dance.
2. Self-injurious behavior. People slap themselves, bite their hands and arms, or hit their heads against the wall or floor repeatedly.
3. Aggression. People assault their peers and staff by hitting, kicking, biting, spitting, or throwing objects.
4. Property damage. People engage in destructive behavior ranging

from picking little pieces out of the chair or shredding their clothes, to breaking windows and furniture or tearing doors off hinges.

MAXIM: *Idle hands are the devil's workshop.*

Toolbox
Supported Routine Outcomes

Facilitates Connections – Forms Relationships
Maximizes Independence – Minimizes Intrusions
Enhances Self Worth – Produces Self Determination (Control)

These are all behaviors that you will likely observe in any setting that denies people the opportunity for active involvement and participation with their environment. These behaviors are almost always present in settings designed to serve Outsiders, e.g., state hospitals, nursing homes, juvenile detention centers (with some stylistic differences depending on the population). It is, therefore, reasonable to conclude that behaviors such as those listed above are not characteristic of any particular group of Outsiders. Though it is embarrassing to admit it, I used to believe that they were characteristics of a particular group of Outsiders; that such behaviors were symptoms of a person's diagnosis.

Seldom, however, is there genetic damage, brain dysfunction or other diagnostic entities that cause people to act this way. You may notice striking similarities when you visit a large residential facility for people with mental illness, one for elders, or one for children who have no parents. You can observe, to varying degrees, the four alternative behaviors in all of these settings. In light of such similarity of behavior, we need to re-examine our stereotypes and come to an almost inescapable new realization. These behaviors occur in places where there is limited opportunity to be actively involved in one's life, regardless of the attributes of the people who live there.

TALE

My TV

I visited a home in which three young men were living. Randy, one of the men, indicated by gestures and vocalizations that he wanted me to see something in his bedroom. I entered Randy's room, and he pointed with pride at a brand new 13-inch television set on a table. He kept saying, "My TV. My TV," all the while smiling broadly. I found out later that Randy had purchased the TV with money he had saved from his sheltered workshop income over a period of six months. That TV was his most prized possession.

A couple of months later, I returned to Randy's home. I remembered the new TV, and I asked him about it. He got a sad expression on his face and shook his head in a gesture of negation. One of the staff told me that Randy had gotten angry one evening and smashed his TV set against the bedroom wall.

Why, I wondered, would someone destroy his own property, something he had worked and saved for? The answer, I believe, has to do with the issue of control. There was always one thing he could do to assert himself as somebody. He could smash his own prized TV set out of sheer frustration and rage at a life that allowed little in the way of options and no constructive way to influence his destiny.

This condition of having limited opportunities and options for meaningful interactions with people and objects in one's life is sometimes referred to as anomie. Literally, anomie means "no law, or no name." It comes from the same root as the word anonymous. People who suffer from anomie have no investment in their lives or the lives of the people around them. They do not have the relationships that constitute the warp and woof of the community life. They act out the conclusion, "If my life has no meaning or value, I will behave in a way to cause your life to have no meaning or value either."

> **MAXIM:** *If my life has no meaning or value, I will behave in a way to cause your life to have no meaning or value either.*

We have seen examples of anomie in recent historical events. People who live in a bleak inner-city moonscape of empty buildings and empty lives, who have no opportunity to control their destinies, may act out their anomie by burning and looting. As a society, we are used to thinking of the causes of such behavior being poverty or lack of education or violence in the streets. Could it be that the real root of such violent self-destructiveness is an almost total lack of the kinds of options many people take for granted? Adolescents who live in areas of urban blight don't think about what they will be when they grow up; they wonder if they will grow up.

Likewise, people who live in bleak institutional environments, whose lives are regimented, directed, programmed, and devoid of meaningful options, have little reason to care about the long-range planning strategies necessary for putting together a meaningful life. This is why many of the behavior management plans generated by psychologists don't work. They don't speak to the need for a person to have an impact on his or her own life, to make choices and be somebody.

> **MAXIM:** *You can't fix a broken life with a Behavior Management Plan (BMP).*

Indeed, among the disciplines that are generally present in services for Outsiders, it is social work which most commonly addresses the needs for autonomy and relationships. If anomie is the cause of challenging behavior, a good social work approach may be the best solution. People who are active participants in their lives are more likely to form meaningful relationships and gain things of value–hobbies, collections, spirituality, employment. It is by experiencing valued relationships and things of value that people can avoid a life of anomie. Through these experiences a person is building the foundation to realize his or her preferred future and proclaim "I am somebody."

MAXIM: *If we were all good social workers, we wouldn't need psychologists.*

The Quality of Life Profile is a device for assessing and evaluating lifestyles. By plotting on a graph the activities you spend your time on and considering both the relative value and the importance of personal relationships in those activities, you can gain insight into the style of your life. Are you a solitary individual, preferring to do things alone? Or are you a gregarious, social person to whom relationships with others are an important part of what is valuable in an activity? Do you have lots of activities in your life that are highly valued, or relatively few activities of limited importance? Are you pleased with your lifestyle? Where on the graph would you like to be? How are you going to get there?

Try helping an Outsider generate his or her profile. Does Outsider status tend to put a person in a particular quadrant? Do people who live with institutional characteristics even have a lifestyle? How does your lifestyle compare with theirs? What activities, events, or opportunities could you support that would help a person enhance their quality of life?

UNIVERSAL ENHANCEMENT
Quality of Life Profile

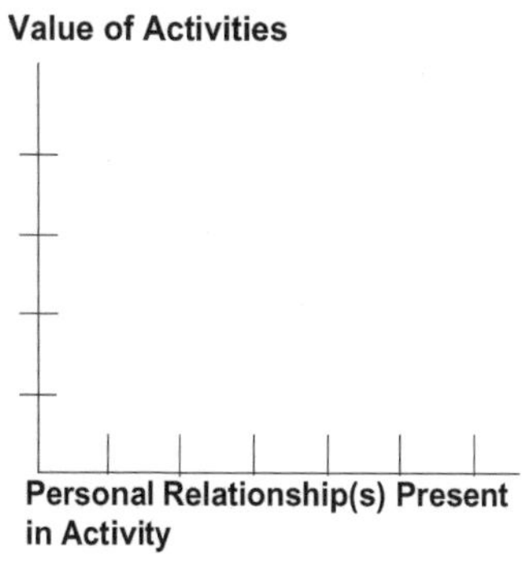

Activities of Value:

1. Classical Music
2. Gardening
3. Dining Out
4. Fishing
5. Camping
6. Baseball
7. Antiqueing
8. Action/Mystery Videos
9. Public Speaking
10. Shopping
11. Writing
12. Travel
13. Walking

Instructions

Think about the things that you like to do, the activities that bring you personal satisfaction, fulfillment and joy. Now place each activity somewhere on the Quality of Life Profile, following the instructions below.

The Quality of Life Profile has two scales. On the left (abscissa), progressing from bottom to top, is the scale of the value of your life activities. Those activities you most value would be noted at the top, while less valued pastimes would be designated near the bottom. Across the bottom (ordinate), is the scale for the personal relationships involved. An activity you do alone, like reading a magazine or collecting stamps, belongs toward the left-hand side of the line. Something you do with friends, like playing volleyball or going dancing, belongs toward the right-hand side of the line. The scale across the bottom answers the question: How important are relationships with other people in this activity?

Use a combination of the two factors to plot each of your chosen activities. If an activity is of low interest and you are indifferent to the presence of other people in the activity, it goes in quadrant C. If, however, you want to record something that is very valuable to you, and the relationships it brings are part of that value, place it in quadrant B.

There is no right answer to this profile; it is not a test. It is a task for self-exploration, designed to give you a picture of what kind of life you have.

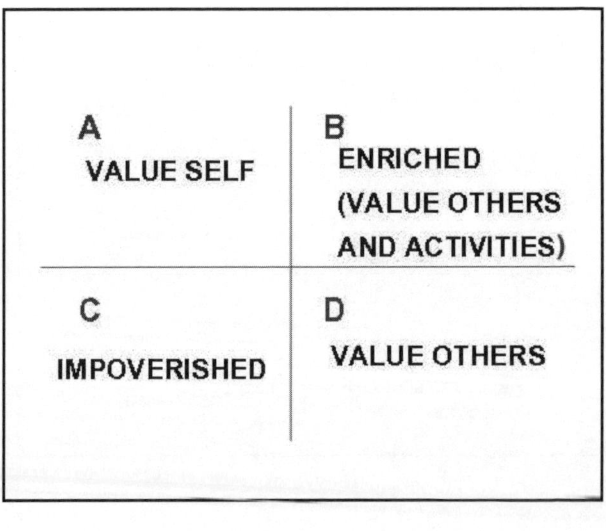

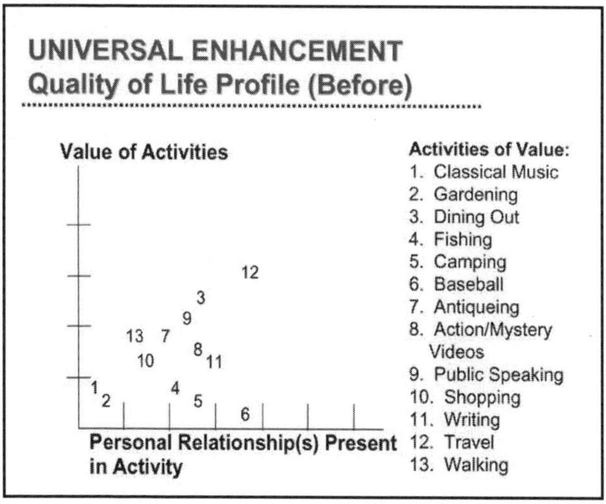

Shown in the examples are completed profiles depicting an individual's quality of life prior to and subsequent to life-enhancing opportunities.

Habilitation = Participation = Universal Enhancement

The usual method of habilitation in an institutional setting is to create places and scheduled times where there is media and the opportunity to interact with it. One response is to design activities of daily living (ADL) rooms, which have the materials for learning to set a dining

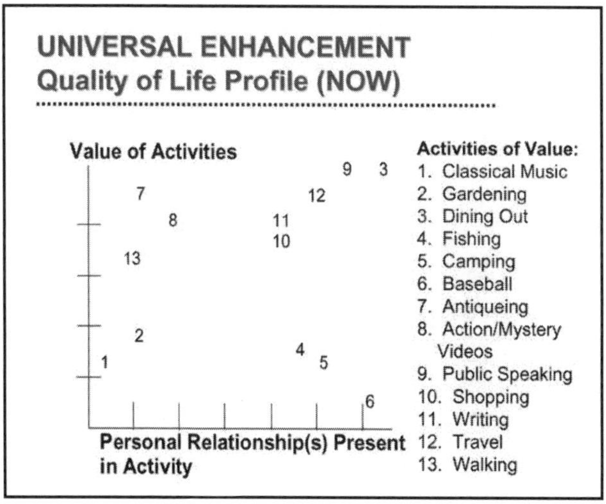

table, do laundry, or prepare a simple meal. The idea is that once the person learns how to perform these tasks in the training room, he or she will be allowed to exercise them in his or her residence. When they can consistently and safely demonstrate all requisite skills in the constructed living area, they can then move from their present residence out to a less restrictive environment, where the media for learning are not locked up or broken.

What is often not recognized here is that movement to a less restrictive environment does not necessitate an actual physical move from one place to another. A less restrictive environment is not a place; it is, rather, an expansion and enhancement of the opportunities and options in a person's life. It is time for everyone to move out, right now. There are no skill acquisition prerequisites to having the opportunity to have a life. It is difficult to learn new skills any place other than where those skills are generally needed as part of a life that has meaning and dignity–a life of Universal Enhancement.

Universal Enhancement, like habilitation, is a result of participation in one's own life and the life of the community in which one lives. Universal Enhancement can be applied to any setting and level of ability. It is culture free and location free. It is a tool to maximize anyone's quality of life. Let's take a closer look at how this interaction with media can become the foundation for Universal Enhancement. The following eight characteristics have been identified as core or primary characteristics for ensuring a solid foundation for Universal Enhancement. There are many other characteristics, but these are the most important.

Functional

The supported routines must have a function and a purpose. That purpose is to enhance competence and increase one's ability to adapt to and manage one's environment. The person who waves a shoelace in front of his face all day (stereotypical behavior) is certainly engaged with media. But he learns no adaptive skills from this engagement; the activity is not functional. Skill acquisition in and of itself does not necessarily increase a person's ability to adapt to his environment.

Universal Enhancement Tools

The Tools of Universal Enhancement Are:

- ⋆**FREE - not available for purchase.**
- ⋆**May be utilized without permission of others**
- ⋆**Consistent with existing regulations, policies and procedures**

TALE

Bertha Reaches Out

Bertha had a stroke, which limited her range of motion and her ability to walk independently. A physical therapist prescribed daily range of motion exercises, and staff helped Bertha obtain a walker to help her in ambulating about her home. The interdisciplinary team had set vacuuming rugs as a training goal for Bertha for the coming year, but because of Bertha's physical limitations, they decided to postpone this goal until she had better motor abilities.

A staff person who provided support to Bertha for a number of years suggested that instead of deferring the training in vacuuming, the team should let it serve as the physical therapy. "When Bertha reaches out with the vacuum cleaner to clean under the couch, she's doing the same thing as those exercises the physical therapist gave her. Why can't she get her exercise by doing the vacuuming?" she asked.

This alert staff person knew that the best way to develop functional skills is by participating in meaningful activities that require those skills. But there's more to the story. The staff person also realized that the real

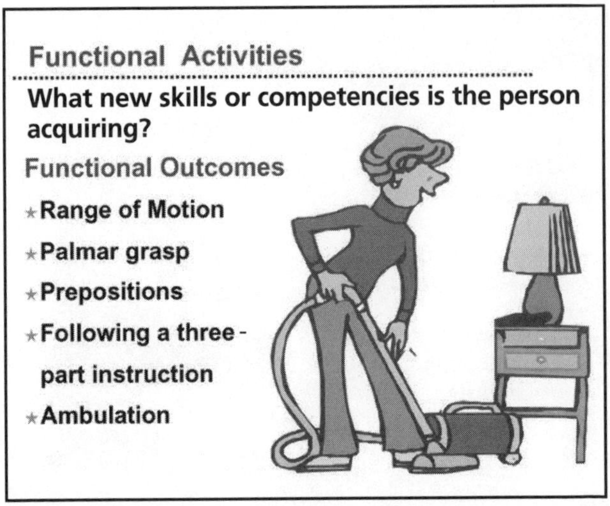

reason Bertha needed to increase her range of motion was so she could use her walker more efficiently. And the real reason she wanted to learn to use her walker more efficiently was so she could go shopping with her sister.

Meaningful

It used to be a joke about basic military training that the drill sergeant would have new recruits go out to a field and dig holes, then fill them in again. Was the individual engaged with various media? Of course. The recruit was engaged with the shovel, the dirt, and the sergeant. Was it functional; did it teach new skills? Certainly. The recruit could learn how to angle the shovel to get the best dirt load, and how far to throw that load so it wouldn't fall back into the hole. He could build his upper body strength and his endurance. He might even learn what happens if he doesn't follow the sergeant's orders! The task is certainly functional. But the recruit is probably wondering how meaningful it is.

Outsiders, (people like recruits) are not seen as peers or equals to those who set task expectations. They are often required to engage in activities that have little meaning. Consider the fraternity pledge's chore of scrubbing the kitchen floor with a toothbrush or the tenderfoot Boy Scout's errand to find a "smoke bender."

The test of whether or not the training task is meaningful is to ask the question, "If the person who is engaged in the task was not doing this task, would someone else have to do it?" In other words, is this a real task, or is it just made up for training purposes?

MAXIM: *If the person who is engaged in the task was not doing it, would someone else have to do it?*

Some disability training equivalents of the soldier's hole digging are "beads on a string," "rings on a stick," and "pegs in a pegboard." In the latter task, the person is given a flat board with rows of holes in it and a box of pegs that fit into the holes. They are then required to put the pegs into the holes.

Now this task does indeed have many potential functional outcomes. The "pegger" can improve eye-hand coordination, pincer grasp, sequencing, color recognition, attention to task, work endurance, following instructions, and on and on. But is it a real task? If the person being trained were not doing it, would a pegboard technician have to come in and make sure all the pegboards are filled? Of course not.

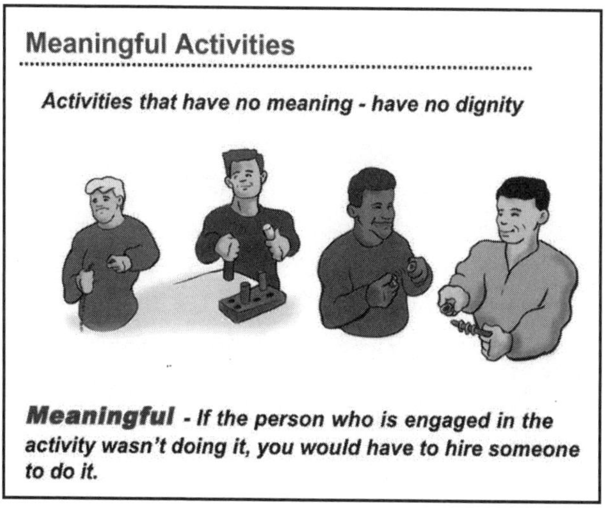

Pegboard filling does not meet the criterion for meaningfulness. And the proof of that is that when the person finishes the task, the pegs are removed from the pegboard, put back in the box, and the "pegger" gets to do the task all over again. To add to the tragedy their work is usually destroyed in front of them. How would you feel if someone came and destroyed your work when you were finished? You'd probably think, "This is stupid." You'd probably resist doing it. Then you'd end up with an "increase on-task behavior" goal on your next IHP.

Giving people meaningless undertakings is demeaning and disrespectful, and it should come as no surprise that people who are subjected to these activities rebel against them in the best way they know how. Tasks that have no meaning have no dignity. Rebellious behavior may be a person's means of communicating the plea: Treat me with dignity.

Instead of making up meaningless training activities, let's use all of the real, everyday tasks that are readily at hand. Eye-hand coordination can be learned by setting the table. Pincer grasp can be improved by holding a toothbrush. Raking the leaves in the front yard can increase work endurance.

MAXIM: *Tasks that have no meaning have no dignity.*

When skills are taught through participation in real tasks, we don't have to worry about "generalization," the concern about whether the person can apply the newly learned skill to novel situations (in various environments). This concern is only valid if the skill is being learned in an environment different from that in which it is to be applied (learning to dress in a training room, for instance). Meaningful skills are being applied at the time they are being learned.

TALE

My Brother Daryl

My brother, Daryl, has severe mental retardation. He has been in school for 12 years and has never been served in any setting other than an elementary school. He has had years of "individualized instruction." He can do lots of things he couldn't do before!

He can put 100 pegs in a board in less than ten minutes while in his seat with 95% accuracy...

But he can't put quarters in vending machines.

Upon command, he can touch nose, shoulder, leg, foot, hair, ear. He is still working on wrist, ankle, hips...

But he can't blow his nose when needed.

He can do a 12-piece Big Bird puzzle with 100% accuracy and color an Easter Bunny and stay in the lines...

But he prefers music and was never taught how to use a radio or tape player.

He can fold primary paper in halves and, even, quarters...

But he can't fold his clothes.

He can sort blocks by colors–up to 10 different colors...

But he can't sort clothes, whites from colors, for washing.

He can roll Play-Doh and make wonderful clay snakes...

But he can't roll bread dough and cut out biscuits.

He can string beads in alternating colors and match it to a pattern on a DLM card...

But he can't lace his shoes.

He can sing his ABCs and tell me names of all the letters of the alphabet when presented on a card in upper case with 80% accuracy...

But he can't tell the men's room from the ladies' when we go to a restaurant.

He can be told it's cloudy/rainy and take a black felt cloud and put it on the day of the week on an enlarged calendar, without assistance...

But he still goes out in the rain without a raincoat or hat.

He can identify with 100% accuracy 100 different Peabody Picture Cards by pointing...

But he can't order a hamburger by pointing to a picture or gesturing.

He can walk a balance beam frontward, sideways, and backward... But he can't walk up the steps of the bleachers unassisted in the gym or go to a basketball game.

He can count to 100 by rote memory...

But he doesn't know how many dollars to pay the waitress for a $2.59 McDonald's special.

He can put a cube "in" the box, "under" the box, "beside" the box, and "behind" the box...

But he can't find the trash bin in the cafeteria and empty his trash there.

He can sit in a circle with appropriate behavior and sing songs and play Duck Duck Goose...

But nobody else his age in our neighborhood seems to want to do that.

I guess he's just not ready yet.

Taken from The Cutting Edge, October 1987. Author unknown.

Normalized rhythm

One of the things learned from the routines of our day is when to begin and end our various tasks. We brush our teeth in the morning or after meals. We flush the toilet after using it. We cook our food just before mealtime. We get dressed when we get up and undressed when we go to bed. Our lives have a rhythm, a context, a logical sequence. One activity or event triggers initiation of the next.

When we teach people tasks at training time, a time that is chosen because of scheduling needs rather than a response to the rhythms of life, we do not allow them to learn the flow and pace of daily events. Such an approach inhibits the recognition of the interconnectedness of activities and tasks, that the occurrence of one event leads to something else happening. We go to bed, for instance, because we are sleepy or because our work is done or because we have to get up early for work in the morning or because the TV news is over, not because it's 8:30 p.m.–bedtime on the master schedule. The "by the clock" approach is not only demeaning–in that we wouldn't impose a rigid schedule on someone we considered to be our equal–it is also counterproductive. When we do not assist people to learn the rhythm of things, we will always have to schedule and prompt them, keeping them dependent on us.

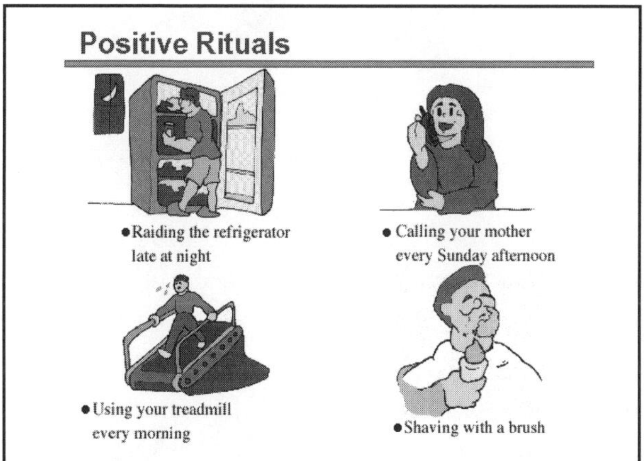

Supporting others in developing positive rituals enhances the quality of life.

One aspect of the learned helplessness seen in many people who have lived for years in institutional settings is that they stop self-initiating. They are so accustomed to being scheduled according to the convenience of staffing patterns, that they have never learned to schedule themselves according to the flow of a daily routine. When the rhythms of an individual's life are determined by paid staff or concerned caretakers, the tail is wagging the dog.

Age appropriate

This issue is dealt with in more depth in Chapter 3, but it's important to consider some of the ramifications of using age-appropriate media

The Tail Should Not Wag the Dog

when we're trying to achieve habilitative outcomes through a level of engagement.

If the media, the *stuff*, used for teaching adults new tasks is the kind that young children commonly use, we will almost certainly limit our expectations of what the person can do. For example, we have seen some people with intellectual disabilities produce fine, expressive paintings using oil paints on canvas. What would we have seen if we had only allowed them to use a Beauty and the Beast coloring book and some crayons? Wouldn't we probably have been concerned with staying in the lines and the color of the sky? If we are complaisant about Joe, at age 27 playing with a stuffed dinosaur, will we be likely to take the time to help him learn how to operate a cassette player?

Adults generally have a larger set of options than children do. When we surround an adult who has limited competence with the kinds of things an adult usually has access to, he will learn how to use those things. He may develop the skills and competencies he needs for a more satisfying life.

We should not settle for a perpetual childish game of pretend, but rather make sure we enrich a person's environment with real things that have real uses.

Participates as equals

We need a vision of "teaching" that goes beyond the model of the teacher walking around the room giving instructions to students. Our new vision is one of full participation (modeling) as the key to learning. If "students" are doing real tasks, with real media, at the appropriate time they should be conducted, then we should all be more than willing to participate as equals with the people we are supposedly teaching. Only when we are trying to get people to do things that are silly and meaningless will we not want to be involved.

MAXIM: *Don't take people for a walk. Walk with them.*

Once again we are faced with the distinction between teaching and providing opportunities to learn. We provide opportunities by supporting people who are learning how to do new things, giving them just as much support and assistance as they need, but no more. We need to serve as role models, participating with people in order to know how it should be done, rather than standing back in the role of instructor.

When working in residential settings, support staff should sit down

at the table and eat with the people who live there. This allows the staff to model appropriate mealtime behavior, including the wonderful communicative interaction that can take place around the dinner table. Mealtime is an opportunity to share, give, take, and review the activities of the day. None of the fine stories would take place if the staff were posted like guards or waiters around the perimeter of the dining room, waiting for the chance to catch someone spilling their milk or stealing a biscuit from their neighbor.

Ultimately, the level of participation that should be seen is complete inclusion in a vital community, where natural supports (unpaid friends, neighbors and coworkers) prevail and there is no need for paid staff. We can initiate that process of minimizing the distinction between trainer and trainee, teacher and student, staff and client. The barriers between people will tumble, as we participate in all activities of life as equals with people we support.

In the appropriate environment

Different events and activities take place in different locations. We get dressed in the bedroom, brush our teeth in the bathroom, cook in the kitchen, vacuum where the dirt is. We learned these tasks by seeing others do them and by being given the opportunity to participate in them.

Environments are rich with cues that tell us how and when to act. When we stand at the crosswalk at a busy intersection, for example, we see and hear not only the walk/don't walk signs but also the other people. We see them crossing or not crossing and looking in the direction in which they expect to see traffic. We see the traffic stopping or turning, the driver slowing for a turn and gesturing us to cross ahead of him. This multiplicity of events, each one containing some information relevant to whether it is safe for us to cross, cannot be duplicated by the erection of a fake traffic light on an institutional back street. Nor is it duplicated by the selection of the walk symbol from a collection of cardboard training tools presented in the dining room during the pedestrian safety training program.

It is not surprising that people who train others in fake environ ments wonder whether the person will generalize the skill in a natural environment. When the surroundings in which training occurs are contrived and artificial, a person who has difficulty learning will often be overwhelmed by the cues that are present in any real world situation. We may then wonder why the person who performed so well during their training program using the shopping trip board game wanders off in a daze during a trip to the mall.

Another reason for learning skills in the environment in which they are to be practiced is that people with intellectual disabilities often have difficulty discriminating subtle distinctions between environments. For instance, if it is deemed acceptable for a man to walk out of the bathroom at this group home with his pants around his knees while attempting to find someone in the living room to help him pull them up, he might think it is appropriate to do the same thing when he walks out of the bathroom at McDonald's or the library.

The most effective way the people we support can learn that there are definite places for different activities is for them to learn those activities in those places. That is, teach the skill in the environment where it is to be exercised. We do no favors by teaching people how to cook in fake kitchens at the day program or how to dress in a classroom. The

A Level of Engagement Becomes Habilitation When it Meets These Eight Characteristics:

- **Functional**
- **Meaningful**
- **Normalized rhythm**
- **Age appropriate**
- **Staff participate as equals**
- **Conducted in appropriate environment**
- **Individual participates from beginning to end**
- **The engagement must be consequated**

environments in which we live, work, and play contain many rich and subtle cues to which all of us have learned to respond. People with intellectual disabilities need to learn to respond in a similar fashion, under similar conditions.

MAXIM: *Teach the skill in the environment where it is to be exercised.*

Engaged in from the beginning of the task/event to the end

The necessity of dealing with this issue is a remnant of the old backward chaining training technique. If the person we were working with was on Step 3 of her dusting program–"applies rag to tabletop in circular fashion"–we used to gather all the materials required, spray the cleaning compound on the table, hand the trainee the rag, and say, "Dust the table, Eleanor." When she met the stipulated criterion, she would then be allowed (ready) to move on to the next step–"sprays cleaning compound to table." It might be a while before she is permitted to "gather materials."

As noted in the previous volume, total task learning is preferred. It is complete immersion in the entirety of any activity. It is crucial that the person who is learning a new skill learn the whole skill, from beginning to end. Eleanor has the right to participate in the total task. Not only will she possibly need to dust her own table someday and need to know how to do it independently, but in addition, every task presents opportunities for functional learning that should not be missed (e.g., ambulation, pincer grasp, eye-hand coordination, letting go). For instance, if Eleanor has limited use of her hands, taking the cap off the sprayer, pointing it in the right direction, pushing down on the button, and letting it go are all occasions for learning. We should not turn our backs on the wealth of learning opportunities contained in what appears to be a simple task.

A final reason for total task learning is that if a person is not participating in the task, they are probably waiting for someone to do it for them.

Water In Your Well

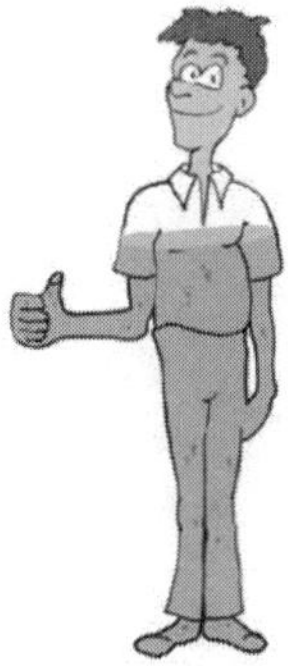

When your well is full - there is much to give.

Waiting is not a meaningful life activity, yet many people who live in institutional settings spend a good deal of their time doing just that–waiting for dinner, waiting for a bath, waiting for bedtime–waiting for someone else to implement one's life. People who are waiting are being deprived, often by well-meaning staff who still see themselves as caretakers, of opportunities to participate in the activities of their own lives.

Consequated

We are all motivated by appreciation of our efforts by significant others. Everyone needs to know that they're really doing a good job, that their effort is valued, and that their willingness to try, maybe to fail, is recognized. This is particularly true of people whose natural curiosity and ambition have been sapped by the enervating anonymity of the institutional crowd. Such anonymous Outsiders, especially, need some message that they are somebody, that they have value in this world. Therefore, every supportive routine must include the message that the person completed the task, did well or made a good attempt, and is appreciated and valued.

Some people, though, experience serious personal difficulty in their attempts to offer praise. They may have grown up in households where praise was withheld and scolding and shaming were the rule of

the day. They may carry a constant voice within them (one that may sound remarkably like a parent) that says, "It's not perfect. She doesn't deserve praise." People who were not praised as children often have great difficulty praising their own children, and the cycle continues from generation to generation (transgenerational). It is important to realize, though, that we have to have "water in our wells" if we are going to be able to praise another person for a job well done, or even a good attempt. If we are insecure, feel unworthy, don't get enough recognition for ourselves, it is very difficult to give out the needed consequation. It is imperative, if you find yourself in this tragic circumstance, that you praise anyway, especially if it is difficult for you. You can always "fake it 'til you make it"–pretend that you feel good about yourself. Recognizing and celebrating the strivings of another person can generate new feelings of self-esteem in you. When you share with the people you support, you will be taking a giant step along the path of Universal Enhancement.

MAXIM: *Fake it 'til you make it.*

If we are not hampered by a transgenerational lack of appreciation,

we are probably accustomed to offering opportunities and praising even small attempts when we spend time with the children in our lives. When my daughter was little, I took her outside to teach her how to shoot a basketball through the hoop. The first time she tried, she just kind of threw the ball in the air, not even in the direction of the basket. I did not say, "Amy, that's not the way; you're not even facing the right direction!" I said, "Amy, that's wonderful. You threw the basketball!" I praised what was her best effort. Don't worry that the person didn't do the whole task or didn't do it perfectly. We can take what we can get closest to what we want. We all have to start somewhere. There's nothing complicated about such praising of successive approximations. We need only present opportunities and then be willing to support people as their independent participation is enhanced a little bit at a time. We meet the person where they are and join with them in a collaborative effort. We are not judging them by some arbitrary pattern of perfection. We are rather working with them, in a relationship of reciprocity and equality. If people waited until whatever we did was excellent before we received praise, we would never be motivated enough to finally accomplish anything.

If we attend to all eight of these characteristics, if we learn them by

heart and apply them with energy and diligence, we will be astounded every day by the difference we can make in the lives of people who have much to learn, ourselves included.

Too Much Time

How, you may ask, are we supposed to accomplish all of these things in those congregate and highly regulated settings in which we are called upon to offer supports? Haven't we set some very high expectations for ourselves and the people we support?

First, we need to be sure the setting in which we work (and in which Outsiders have to live) are rich with the media of life, that all the stuff of daily living is not locked away in the interest of safety, efficiency, or staff convenience.

Second, we must remember that, in settings designed to help people participate more in their lives, time is our enemy. This is not because we don't have enough time to accomplish all that must be done. It is, rather, because we rush through chores and meals, taking over household tasks from the people who are rightfully responsible for them, succumbing to the thinking that we can't afford to be slowed down by the people we support and teach. Once we finish all of our chores, we find we have too much time and no meaningful way to fill it. We may then try to come up with meaningful activities for the remaining time.

Many of us may succumb to the feeling that there is not enough time to "get everything done." Then the people we support, excluded from the meaningful tasks we have just taken from them, have time on their hands. And if they fill that time by engaging in inappropriate behaviors, we–lacking an appreciation of the result of idle hands–will call in the psychologist to set up a behavior management program (which will become another task that "takes up all our time").

MAXIM: *Time is our enemy... because we have too much and no meaningful way to fill it.*

Our answer to the problem of time hanging heavily on people whose repertoire of independent activities is limited, is to take the time to assist the people we support to do things for themselves. We need to be constantly aware of all the possible meaningful learning opportunities that are at their disposal simply by engaging in the tasks of daily living, the activities of everyday life.

Toolbox

Making the Use of Time Meaningful

Home Chores–Everyone we serve and support should be given the opportunity to spend time doing chores in their home, whether they live in their own apartment or share a room in a "residence with 50 other people." These chores can include such tasks as sweeping the sidewalks, mowing the lawn, washing the dishes (or the car), balancing the checking account, shampooing the carpets, taking out the trash, replacing the batteries in the emergency flashlight–as well as the commonly seen "tooth brushing," "bed making," and "vacuuming."

Home chores increase a person's skills, while at the same time increasing that person's investment in their living environment and improving cooperation with house mates and support staff. It instills ownership and pride in one's property and home.

Work–Everyone should have the opportunity (indeed, the right) to engage in meaningful work for eight hours a day, five days a week (not "day program" or "vocational activities," but real work, productive tasks that would have to be done if that person weren't doing them). Work has always been the great equalizer for disenfranchised people of all sorts, whether recent immigrants or racial minorities or women. People who work feel good about themselves and are recognized as valuable contributors to society. People who work earn money that brings them options in how and where to live, options for self-determination. Work empowers.

MAXIM: *Work is a great equalizer. It promotes dignity and respect.*

Dining–Mealtimes should not be a 20-minute "scarf" and go. They should be rich occasions not just for learning mealtime skills, like using a fork or a napkin, but for developing communication skills, building relationships and savoring the flavors. There is no reason why meals shouldn't be served in three courses, with the table cleared between service. Supper could take two hours. Why not? There's not enough time?

Volunteering–Many people spend quality time doing volunteer work in their communities. We feel good about ourselves as we give of our time, talent and attention. In addition, we build new relationships with people who have similar interests. People with disabilities also need this experience of being someone who has something to give.

MAXIM: *People with intellectual disabilities have been on the receiving end of giving far too long.*

Leisure–We cherish our leisure time. We love to fill it with events that relax and fulfill us. We like to spend time with our friends, try new activities, see new places. Outsiders, on the other hand, are often relegated to spending their time waiting for something to happen or are forced to participate in meaningless time-fillers, such as going on a van ride.

Home Chores-It's Their Right

Actively participating in home chores:

- **Proclaims this is my home and I am a responsible person**
- **Provides for a meaningful level of engagement**
- **Facilitates the acquisition of new skills**
- **Enhances self-worth**
- **Promotes independence**

Assure that each resident has the opportunity to engage in a minimum of 20 hours of home chores per week.

Free Time

"But what about free time?" you might ask. "It sounds like you want to fill people's every waking hour with tasks from which they can learn. Shouldn't they have time to just kick back and relax?" The answer is yes, of course they should. There is one caveat: people with disabilities (indeed, all people) have no right to free time...to engage in inappropriate behavior. They do not need time in which to shred their shirts or beat their heads against the wall or assault their neighbor or drink themselves into oblivion.

MAXIM: *People do not have the right to free time... to engage in inappropriate behavior.*

Free Time

The people we support have no right to free time… to engage in inappropriate behavior.
Time is our enemy because they have too much of it and not a meaningful way to use it.

"Wait" is a vulgar word. What are they waiting for?
***They are waiting* for lunch.**
***They are waiting* for their medication.**
***They are waiting* to go to their day program.**
***They are waiting* to go to bed.**
***They are waiting* to take a bath.**
***They are waiting* to have a life.**

The amount of free time a person should have is determined by their ability to use it.

Once again, this maxim does not apply just to people with disabilities. It is relevant to all people who, because of limited options and lack of skill, can find no constructive occupation of their time. It is universal. It applies to elderly people living in nursing homes and young people hanging out on street corners.

We do have an obligation, moral and professional, to help people learn constructive uses of their free time. And we do that the same way we teach any other skill–by providing media, the opportunity, and the assistance and support each person needs to develop their competency in making choices for their use of leisure time.

The more competence a person demonstrates, the larger the set of options that can be offered for free time. That set may include just sitting under a tree watching the clouds pass overhead, but not while urinating in his pants. It may include watching television, but not while pinching his neighbor. People who make an informed choice, from among acceptable options of what to do with their leisure time, can do virtually anything they want to do in their non-work time. It is our job to support and assist people in reaching the place where their options are limited neither by lack of competency nor by lack of opportunity.

Relationships

If relationships are the task at hand, what kind of media can we use? In the formation of relationships, people are the media. Those of us who work professionally to support and assist people are paid for our relationships. Our task is to make introductions, to help people who have been isolated from the mainstream of society because of their differences to come to know and interact with "the butcher, the baker, the candlestick maker." Recall the maxim: If we were all good social workers, we wouldn't need psychologists. Many people consider the interaction with other human beings amongst the most meaningful events in their lives.

Resistance

I often hear, "Ed doesn't want to do his training program." That communicates to me that the characteristics elaborated above are present. Maybe the task is not meaningful to the individual. Maybe it's not being scheduled at a time appropriate or desired by the individual. It could be that the staff are not participating but are standing over the person, supervising–doing *to*. Or there may just not be a good enough payoff at the end of the task–inadequate consequation (compensation). Or that person may not value the task. So the person being trained asks, rightly, "Why should I bother?"

If training is actually presenting real opportunities for inclusion and participation, there is usually no motivation problem. People want to learn the things that will assist them in developing new relationships and in participating in activities that bring them pleasure and joy. People want to learn skills that will free them from the intrusiveness of having others in their space and in their face providing supports. If we are keeping people from these opportunities, getting them "ready" by teaching them new skills, we will have to provide artificial motivation. If we use the stuff that surrounds real people in real environments, if that is our training equipment, we will soar through skill acquisition and get on to the real task at hand, the development of meaningful relationships.

What if we would all learn and use the eight characteristics of turning supported routines into Universal Enhancement; if we would ask, show and assist in all our engagements and always strive not to do things alone; if we would think out loud and take what we can get closest to what we want? The places in which we support and serve people would become places in which all of us grow, develop, and increase the quality of our lives (Universal Enhancement), instead of schools in which students prepare for some future life that is held out to be available when they're "ready."

2

Turning Obstacles into Opportunities

I sometimes hear objections to implementing the principles and values of Universal Enhancement, and they usually start something like, "Well, that's all a great idea, but we can't because..." The critic then recites a list of reasons why the people served must be dealt with differently from what is proposed in Universal Enhancement. Either the people being served have dangerous levels of challenging behavior, or they lack the skills, or they have serious medical issues, or the community won't accept them, or there's not enough money, or the surveyors wouldn't like it, or the parents don't support it, or there's not enough staff... and on and on. Anyone who has worked with Outsiders or disenfranchised persons for any length of time has heard, and probably used, many of the available excuses.

My response is to turn the critic's opposition into a personal challenge. The reasons you give why it can't be done are the justification for doing it. At first, this appears to be a facile rejoinder; but if we look more deeply, we see that it is a guide for helping us balance the sometimes conflicting demands of opportunity and protection.

MAXIM: *The reasons you give why it can't be done are the justification for doing it.*

Let's start with a simple example. Why isn't there a salt shaker on the dining room table at suppertime? The reason given is that Susie is on a diet prescribed by her physician that prohibits added salt. That's exactly why the salt has to be there–so Susie can learn that she needs to use the salt substitute. Susie should be given support and assistance as she learns how to choose for herself, but no more help than she truly needs. Transitional support is merely being provided along the way to Susie running her own life.

Why doesn't Joe get to go to the mall? Because the last time he was there, he "pitched a fit," broke a planter, and scared a lot of shoppers. Well, that's why he needs to go on the next trip–so we can help him learn how to shop appropriately at the mall. Offer Joe the opportunity of shopping at the mall, while at the same time assuring that his disruptive and socially inappropriate behaviors are redirected. Help him by providing the supports, assistance and guidance he needs for having an enjoyable and successful shopping trip.

Why doesn't Terry have a key to his house? The reason given is that he will lose it or swallow it. Well, how is he ever going to learn to use a key if he can't have the opportunity to have one until he knows how to use it? We need to accept the challenge to identify and apply creative supports for Terry, so he can have his key to his house. We may

Having a key to your front door proclaims ownership and control

want to help Terry purchase a key chain (like the ones staff members wear). We may decide to help Terry put his key on a plastic paddle device to prevent him from losing or swallowing it (like the kind used at the corner gas station to keep people from putting the restroom keys in their pockets). Or we may need to carry Terry's key for him temporarily, handing it to him as we approach the door. And, we may need to assist him with placing it in the lock, unlocking the door, and returning the key to us for safekeeping. What is clear is that Terry's quality of life is not enhanced by accepting his inappropriate or skill-deficient behavior as a justification for denying him a key to his house.

Reasonable Risks – A Question of Balance

You may remember from the discussion of the characteristics of the institution that one of those characteristics was the denial of the dignity that results from the opportunity to engage in risky and challenging endeavors. As children, most of us learned important as well as trivial tasks by being allowed, by parents or caretakers, to take reasonable risks. This was done in order to give us the opportunity to develop the skills and understanding that would allow us to rise to a new occasion.

Of course, our parents filtered those risks, not allowing us, for instance, to play in the street for the opportunity of learning about speeding cars. In such a case, the consequences for not having learned the lesson are too dire. Likewise, I do not advocate that you put gasoline in a pitcher on the dining room table, so that Susie can learn not to drink it. But the salt that is not allowed in Susie's salt-free diet will not cause her to drop dead at the dinner table. We, and Susie, must be willing to allow her the potential risk of getting some salt, in order to allow her the opportunity to learn how to control her own salt intake. If Susie is denied this opportunity to participate in and control what at first glance is a trivial element of her own life, she may thereby also be denied the opportunity to eat in a restaurant with her family or go to a friend's house for dinner. She may never be allowed to go places where salt is likely to be on the table and she will be expected to forego its use.

Helping the people we support and assist to choose which risks are "reasonable" and which are unacceptably dangerous is an exacting job. As risk assessors (another form of Gatekeeper), we are like Lady Justice, blindfolded, a balance scale held out in front of us. On one arm of the scale is opportunity/risk; the other is protection. Seeking the right proportion of each element is a tricky task indeed. Come down too far in one direction and we may face charges of carelessness; people's lives may be endangered. Come down too far the other way and we stifle the growth of the people we serve, and we deny them the right to have a life.

Parents whose children live with them usually know their children's abilities well enough to assess which risks are permissible. Many of us know of parents, though, who err on the conservative side; we call them over-protective. And we know of those whose mistaken judgments fall on the overly lenient side; we call them negligent. The same categories can be applied to people who offer supports and assistance to Outsiders.

An important point to bear in mind here is that the assessment of the reasonableness of a particular risk should be based not on the perceived abilities or disabilities of the people we support, but rather on our own ability or inability to provide the needed assistance, protective oversight or environmental safeguards. Seen in this light, the assessment process takes on a whole different aspect. The process includes

an assessment of the environment, adaptations that may be needed, and an evaluation of resources available (including people resources) to support an individual. Our assessment knowledge needs to include an understanding of the unique characteristics of the individual for whom we will be providing support. For instance, deciding whether it is an acceptable risk for Susie to have a salt shaker on her dinner table depends on our assessment of whether or not we can give Susie the supervision she needs for success and safety. Another example is that maybe Joe's response at the mall was because he does not like to be around large crowds of people. Many of us have similar dislikes or discomforts as evidenced by increased anxiety type behaviors around crowded holiday shopping venues. An alternative may be to go at less busy, hectic times.

Professionals, family members and friends who have accepted the responsibility of assisting people to achieve their highest levels of freedom and independence are held accountable for making decisions about the minimum level of support a particular individual needs in a particular situation. Most of the professionally designed and marketed assessment devices provide little assistance or direction in this ominous task. Nor will the regulations that guide much of our behavior provide us with the necessary judgments. The regulations are designed for the protection of categorical masses of people who are seen as needing to be safeguarded–elders, children, people with disabilities. No regulation can help us respond to the idiosyncrasies, sensitivities, hopes, and desires of the myriad individuals we serve.

Turning Obstacles into Opportunities

I have found, in actual practice, that if we will think of every objection as an opportunity for learning, as indicating a challenge to be overcome, we can turn obstacles into opportunities. This kind of challenge keeps us on our toes, keeps us from sanitizing environments to the point that there is not enough real media, not enough of the "stuff" of which real life is constructed. And it also keeps us away from the extremist "right-ist" position; the stance of the supposed advocate who

The Rightist

The "Rightist" frequently hides behind the issue of rights. The pretense of rights allows the "Rightist" to avoid accountability and exposes their inability to support and teach others how to make a choice

is so concerned with the rights and freedoms of the person with disabilities that the right to be free from harm takes a back seat.

TALE

I recently visited a small rest home for the purpose of meeting someone who was considering moving into a new home where supports and services would be provided. As I neared the rest home, I passed a young man standing on the double yellow line of the exit ramp, gesturing to passing vehicles that he wanted a cigarette. He was clearly in danger. The road was remote from any dwellings other than the place I was visiting. When I arrived, I asked the rest home's director about the young man.

"Oh, he stays there all the time," was the director's reply.

"But isn't it dangerous?" I asked.

"Of course it is," was his reply, "but it's his right to be there."

I take strenuous opposition to the director's position. More in line with the concepts of Universal Enhancement would be to provide the opportunity to learn other ways of obtaining cigarettes and of interacting with people. There was neither dignity nor opportunity in this kind of foolish risk-taking. One's rights should not be unnecessarily restricted, but failure to protect from harm or permitting/supporting an individual to take unnecessary risks may be regarded as neglect.

Hierarchy of Responsibility

Though there is no list of acceptable and unacceptable risks, some direction can be provided. We can use the Trilogy of Service Principles introduced in Volume One.

1. Protect from harm
2. Assure dignity and respect
3. Provide learning opportunities

If any of these responsibilities comes into conflict with another, the one with the higher position on the list takes precedence. Thus, we sometimes find ourselves forgoing dignity and respect temporarily in the interest of protecting a person from harm, such as when we use personal restraint or restrictive devices to prevent people from injuring themselves. (Not very dignified, but we try to apply them with respect.) But we will not sacrifice a person's dignity or the respect we have for them in order to achieve some habilitative goal (that is, to teach new

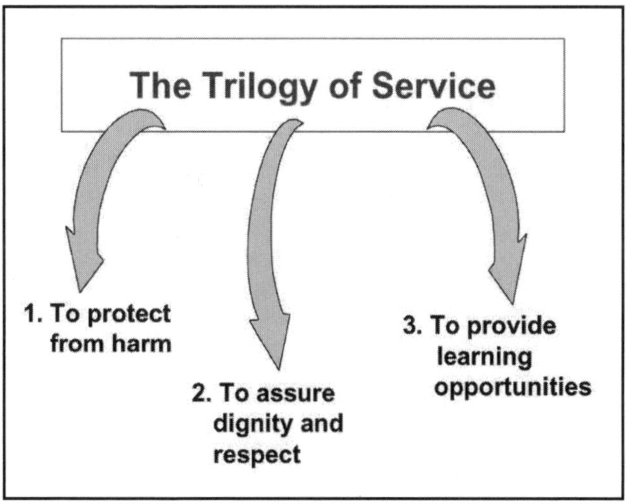

skills) no matter how noble the educational endeavor may seem.

So, does making protection from harm the highest obligation perpetuate the problem in the Medical/Custodial Model, where the doctors and nurses did not let anyone do anything because they were afraid someone might get hurt? The answer lies in a careful definition of protection from harm (also known as protective oversight).

Harm, in this instance, means that individuals would incur substantial injury or damage, physical or emotional, which would take some effort to repair. The focus is not on protecting someone from the reasonable woes and embarrassments of everyday life–the skinned knees, the hurt feelings, the disappointment arising from a failed relationship, or the frustration of not always getting what you want. That sort of excessive concern would indeed lead to the overprotective attitude that causes people to coddle and shelter people who seem unable to negotiate the world on their own. The concern is not only with freedom from harmful, dangerous or uncomfortable circumstances, but also with freedom to be an active participant in life.

When we're wrestling with these decisions it may help to keep in mind the kind of criteria we use in deciding what opportunities to allow ourselves. The risks are weighed against the benefits. If the risk includes a good possibility of real harm, we assess the benefits we would receive from engaging in the activity. When the benefits outweigh the risks, we generally go ahead. This is called enlightened risk.

If a man decides that the imagined benefits of cross-country skiing do not outweigh the risk that his heart condition could cause him to be involved in a severe medical emergency in a remote area, he will abstain. We call this prudence.

It is important to note that the requirement of enlightenment as an element of enlightened risk poses a burden. Those of us who are paid to provide supervision or those family members and friends who have assumed continued responsibility for people who are deemed incapable of making their own judgments of risk must weigh risks and benefits and come to a prudent decision for someone else. When we have responsibility for people with limited judgment, we do not allow them to engage in possibly fatal or damaging activities for the sake of a momentary rush of pleasure (though we do not, interestingly enough, deny ourselves such a rush). Normatives, who live in the world at large, are required to be neither prudent nor reasonable. If we want to engage in bungee jumping, hang gliding, or casual sex because we derive some enormous perceived benefit from these activities, we are allowed to choose to do so, even though they all carry a substantial, and possibly fatal, risk.

We probably will, however, assist the people we support to choose activities which may have a high risk but which nevertheless carry a significant and ongoing benefit. Riding in an automobile, flying in a commercial airplane, and living in a high-rise apartment building are examples of such a choice. These activities, though risky, open up worlds of opportunity for people, and most of us do consider the benefits to be worth the risks involved. At the next level of the hierarchy, we will not do anything in the name of learning opportunities that diminishes our obligation to treat people with dignity and respect. We will not talk to people in a harsh or demeaning way because "they have to learn to listen." We will not subject people to meaningless, repetitive tasks that none of us would do for five minutes just because "it's part of their training program." We will not barge into the bathroom because "we need to keep a record on the BM chart." We will seek to offer people the opportunity to learn new skills, but not at the expense of losing their dignity or self-respect.

Teaching Self-Determination: Choice and Decision-Making

The Trilogy of Service Principles gives us some guidance in knowing how to support people in setting their priorities. But how can we contribute most effectively to their learning to make decisions for themselves? In our day-to-day working with Outsiders, what choices and options are appropriate?

The answer is that we start with a limited set of options and expand the size of that set as the person demonstrates the skills needed to handle more complex decision-making tasks.

For example, to help a man with intellectual disabilities who requires pervasive supports choose the clothes he wants to wear to work that day, you would probably not just open his closet and say, "Max, what do you want to wear to work today?" Max may answer that he wishes to wear the lime green shorts and the lavender T-shirt. On this day, if the forecast calls for a high temperature of 30 degrees with a good chance of freezing rain, you might, instead, offer a choice of two shirts. Both are appropriate for the weather and for Max's work activities, so you ask, "Which shirt do you want to wear today, Max? The blue one or the green one?"

MAXIM: *The more capable a person is, the larger the set of options they are offered.*

Max may make no response, and you may have to help him by lifting his hand and supporting it to touch one of the shirts. But then you will compliment Max for the good choice he made and go on to support Max in choosing a pair of pants from a set that contains two pairs appropriate to the season and the activity.

What you have done here is successfully met the challenge of the reason you give for not doing something is the justification for doing it. You once thought, "Max can't pick out his own clothes. He always picks the wrong colors, and he wants to wear his wool shirt in the summertime." But now you've moved in a creative direction, recognizing that Max's apparent inability to choose appropriate clothes is exactly the justification for the necessity of helping him choose.

As Max's ability to choose increases, you will provide him with more items from which to choose, eventually even including that wool shirt on a summer day. But this time, because you have limited the options for Max, he may have come to know that he'll be a lot more comfortable at work if he chooses a T-shirt. Limiting options is not a denial of rights when it is in support of the right to learn how to make decisions, the right of self-determination.

Normatives may be involved in a similar process when we have to make decisions in an arena where we have limited competence or experience. For example, if a couple is decorating their living room and don't have much color sense, they may hire an interior decorator to present them with a manageable set of options. She probably would not just turn them loose to choose the colors for the curtains. She would say, "Your sofa is blue, and those chairs are green. Here are some colors I think would go well with the furniture." Then she would offer them a limited set of options, each of which could be successful. The couple would be learning to choose colors by being guided by someone who has more experience than they do. The same process holds true for Outsiders. Don't give people choices; teach them to make them.

MAXIM: *Don't give people choices; teach them to make them.*

TALE

Young Dudes Support Choice... and Tom Learns a Lesson

One morning I was visiting a home in North Dakota at 6:30 a.m. I knocked on the door. A very young male employee opened it. I was admittedly prejudiced by this young man's appearance. He was wearing a baseball cap (backwards), and I have some negative feelings about people wearing caps in the house. I looked at his pants and saw a tear in the right knee. I thought, "This is going to be a disaster." Here was this young man who apparently had not worked here very long and who obviously did not know how to present himself in a very favorable light. In my mind, I called him "Dude."

I went inside. The home was unusually quiet. There were four women living there, and all of them used wheelchairs for mobility.

I intended to be an unobtrusive observer, so I quietly walked into the dining room, where the four women were sitting around a table. Another young man in garb similar to Dude's was standing near the table. He had several days unshaven beard growth, further causing my anxiety to arise. I began to think of him as "Beard."

As I watched, Dude approached one of the women and said, "Susan, can I help you go to the kitchen, and we'll get some cereal and bring it back to the table?"

Well, the way that man talked to Susan immediately got my attention. He spoke no louder than was necessary for Susan to hear. He spoke with courtesy and respect. I was impressed.

MAXIM: *Speak no louder than necessary for the person to whom you are speaking to hear you.*

Then, while guiding her hands as necessary, he helped Susan release the brakes of her wheelchair. They went slowly into the kitchen.

The cereal was in a cabinet that was not reachable by a person using a wheelchair. Dude opened the cabinet and said, "Hey, let's get some of these cereals into the dining room." He brought a box of Cheerios halfway down from the cabinet and then assisted Susan in taking the Cheerios the rest of the way down to the tray on her wheelchair. Then, he brought down a box of Grape- Nuts and did the same thing. Then a box of corn flakes. He asked Susan if he could help her return to the dining room.

When they got back to the dining room, Dude helped Susan relock her wheelchair brakes, while Beard walked around the table, quietly assisting the other women.

Dude said to Susan, "May I help you give the cereal to Linda, so she can decide which one she wants for breakfast?"

He helped Susan place each box in a row in front of Linda. Beard came up behind Linda and asked, "Which cereal would you like this morning, Linda?"

Linda took in the row of cereal boxes with an apparently vacant gaze. Then she looked up at Beard. Then she looked back at the cereal. Suddenly, she thrust her arm out and knocked over the box of Cheerios.

Beard seized the occasion and said, "Oh, you'd like Cheerios this morning. May I help you pour some?"

Well, it was obvious to me by now that these two gentlemen fully understood what they were doing. They realized the importance of offering options to support choice-making and they had the personal resources that allowed them to treat those women with the dignity and respect they deserved.

It was I who had fallen short, judging these men by my stereotyping first impression. I should have known better, and I learned much from those young men that cold Dakota morning.

Relationships and Choice

When encouraging and supporting people in making choices in more important and complex life areas than what clothes to wear, the application of the principle of enlightened risk becomes more difficult. We may be forced to make careful judgments about risk factors, benefits and people's current abilities.

For individuals under the aegis of a service system, risk/opportunity decisions are usually based on assessments and goals we have set at some kind of annual planning meeting. There we gather a team of people, so that we can pool our resources and perspectives, in order to make decisions based on enlightened risk. It's a pretty efficient process (and, incidentally, spreads the liability so that no individual gets the blame for a faulty decision), but there's no way we can really get to know a new person in the 30 days we usually have prior to a "staffing." No matter how many professional assessments we administered, how many test scores we accumulated, it would be like trying to buy a meaningful birthday present for someone you just read about in the newspaper, a person you only met once. And here's the nub of the issue: assessing the balance of risks and benefits and deciding on appropriate sets from which to encourage choice making depends on relationship. It depends on knowing something about the person we're supporting and assisting, on knowing that no person is a barrel with limited capacity, on believing deeply that unless someone has an opportunity to take a risk they'll never learn anything.

This kind of relationship, this kind of real knowing of a person, comes more from friends, relatives and the people who provide direct support and assistance than from professionals who have merely administered standardized assessment devices. We may ask, "Do you think Lawrence would like to learn to walk to the store?" The person who works daily with Lawrence, or the friend or family member who has a close relationship with him, is more on the mark saying, "Yeah, I think he'd love to do that, and I think he could do it" than the professional, whose assessment tool may indicate that Lawrence is "not ready" yet.

Relationships, opportunities, choices–these are the essential elements of an environment in which people can grow, learn and become more independent. And these are the cornerstones of Universal Enhancement.

3

"Because We're Not Children Anymore"

Before a final discussion of the elements of Universal Enhancement, a vital issue must be addressed. This issue frequently raises significant emotional reaction, because, unfortunately, it goes to the root of our perceptions of persons with intellectual disabilities and other people who have been disenfranchised. It is the tendency to treat those we believe to be inferior to us as children.

This infantilizing of those who are seen as Outsiders, as not worthy of the respect and courtesy usually accorded adults, pervades nearly all areas wherein people are viewed from a perspective of inequality. This issue arises when African-American adult males are referred to as "Boy," when a 70-year-old woman is called "Sweetie," or when migrant workers are seen as happy campers. It arises anytime adults are treated as and seen as children. Professionals in the field of disabilities services have come to call the issue age appropriateness.

Who is an Adult?

This discussion will begin with a definition that seems almost too obvious to warrant consideration. What constitutes an adult? The answer is simple: adulthood is determined by how long you have lived, not by IQ, nor by physical prowess, academic competence, or life-skills ability. If you are 18 (or 21) years old, you are an adult–period.

MAXIM: *Adulthood is determined only by age.*

People who lack those abilities and skills you would expect them to have, given their years of life experience, are not "children in adult bodies." Nor are they "just like little kids." They are adults who have both strengths/abilities in some areas and skill deficits in other areas, necessitating some level of support and assistance in some of their life activities. In this need for support and assistance, they are no different from Normatives. We all require some degree of support and help in many areas of our lives. Thus, none of us is truly independent; we are all interdependent.

Nothing points up this interdependence more than the large number of specialists in our society who help us with the complicated tasks we don't know how to do or just don't care to do. For instance, I used to change the oil in my car. It was a mark of independence for me to take care of my own needs. Recently, I have started turning the job over to the Fast Way Oil Change down the street. (Their motto is "Let us do your dirty work!") I have not lost any of my manly status by allowing the guys at Fast Way to change the oil. I am not a child because I rely on others for support and assistance. And the Fast Way employees earn their living serving customers in a quick and efficient manner. Fast Way guys and I are now interdependent, an enhancement for both parties.

MAXIM: *None of us are independent; we are all interdependent.*

The prejudicial misperception that people who lack certain abilities are like children is commonly applied to persons who have been demeaned and cast aside because they are not capable, competent, and independent (as all of us imagine ourselves to be). It is not uncommon to hear someone talk to an adult with blindness as if he had to have things spelled out for him simply, the way you would talk to a 5-year-old child. Or a well-meaning neighbor might talk to a woman of 85 as if she had just arrived on the planet and needed the patronizing patience offered to an individual who was unfamiliar with our culture or language.

The notion that adulthood is somehow linked with competence, independence or an expectation of what is "normal" for a certain age is often so deeply ingrained that it is no wonder the least competent people among us are the recipients of the most condescending treatment.

"But We Love Children"

Many people have never taken the time to process their feelings about this issue of treating adult Outsiders like children. If you are a friend, family member, or support person of someone who has disabilities and you really care about them, you may already be asking, "Well, what's wrong with seeing these people as children? I love children, just as I love the person to whom I provide services and support. Being treated as a child is a wonderful life experience. Children are protected from the unpleasantness of life. Children are doted upon and cared for. The life of a child is a wonderful life." Most people would agree with this sentiment. We do, after all, love and cherish our children. We care for them, keep them safe, help them with the things they are unable to do for themselves. When this attitude is applied, however, to aging parents who require nursing services or to adult sons or daughters who have developmental disabilities or to migrant farm workers, we begin to see that being treated as a child, when you are, in fact, an adult, is usually demeaning, disrespectful and limiting. In most cultures we do not–and this is critically important–extend to children the same courtesy and respect and opportunity we unhesitatingly offer to adults.

Respect and opportunity–these are the crucial factors.

Privacy

Let's look at an example of the issue of privacy. Many mothers have no qualms about taking their newly toilet-trained little boys into the women's restroom with them. Many fathers have no problem changing their 1-year-old daughter's diapers on a picnic table at the public park. What would our reaction be were a family member to assist a 40-

year-old woman with her toileting needs in public? Does such a display become acceptable because the woman has the abilities of a 1-year-old, which is to say that she lacks most of the competencies you would expect to see in a woman her age?

Lack of Privacy

In our society, adults are expected to maintain and receive a greater level of personal privacy than are children. An adult who does not protect his own privacy because he has been treated as a child and, therefore, never been taught to be private or to respect the privacy of others, may be shunned as unsocialized, odd, and somehow threatening. Carla, a 2-year-old girl who comes into the living room while her father's assembled friends are playing poker and offers to show an adult acquaintance her new panties is considered cute. Lily, a woman of 30 with intellectual disabilities who does the same thing, is seen as lewd or, even worse, embarrassing, placing her outside the social conventions and mores.

It is crucial that we understand the chain of events here. Some might see Lily as a child in an adult body because she lacks the judgment and ability of the normative woman her age. Those who see her as a child are likely to habitually support behavior that is acceptable in children. Since Lily has not been offered the opportunity to learn adult behavior, she acts like a child. Because she acts like a child, she is perceived as a child.

Lily is caught in a circular trap of our construction. And it is we who must help her escape.

Opportunity

More impacting than the issue of privacy is the matter of opportunity. We do not offer to children the same opportunities for involvement in the community, for participation in activities, for choice and decision making, for initiating relationships that we extend to adults. We justify our limitation of our children's opportunities by the fact that we are responsible to care for them until they grow up, and some opportunities are deemed too risky. As they demonstrate more competence in an area, we offer children more opportunity, even to the extent that we offer them a little more opportunity than they are ready for. That is, we offer them the opportunity to try new things, possibly to fail, almost certainly to grow.

We usually make our decisions about the type of opportunity that we extend by considering the child's age. We expect that a 4-year-old ought to be able to stay overnight at Uncle George's house or a 14-year-old is old enough to go out on a date with a group of age mates. The child may not have demonstrated the requisite competencies for the challenging activity, but we make a judgment based on what we know about her and the expectations we have of what a similar-aged child is likely to be able to do.

Now apply this principle to Sam, age 52, who has an IQ of 58, to see how our expectations for Sam are influenced more by his IQ score than by his age. Sam is single, with no family responsibilities. He works as a janitor at a shoe store four hours a day for a sub-minimum wage arranged by his job coach. He lives in a group home with five other men who also have intellectual disabilities.

On Monday night Sam expresses an interest in going down to the Blue Ribbon Bar and Grill to drink a few beers and watch a football game with some of his coworkers from the store. The staff at the group home are very surprised at this request from Sam, because they perceive Sam as a 10-year-old boy in a gray-headed body. The issues they see as important for Sam's growth and development are his immaturity and lack of social skills. For instance, just last night at dinner Sam had a tantrum after the staff refused to let him take his Ninja Turtles coloring book, which he carries all the time, to the dinner table with him. The staff have been teaching Sam that we don't take our toys to the dinner table. Perceiving Sam as a child, with childish desires and behaviors, no one who provides supports to Sam had ever considered the possibility that he might wish to go to a bar and hang out with some men his own age. How could they have? Seeing and treating Sam as a child, the staff are working on the lessons that children need to learn:

"Don't bring your toys to the table." They are not helping Sam develop a repertoire of adult skills, activities and opportunities which will bring a level of successful participation into his life.

Do you sense what is happening here? The staff who work at Sam's home perceived and treated Sam as a child, because he has an IQ of 58, indicating that he requires intermittent and/or continuous support. Bound by this expectation, the staff were not able to see past their prejudicial attitudes which imposed on Sam an expectation of limited capacity. Sam's support staff is able to offer him the opportunities and alternatives that are usually available to a man his age only if they are able to get past their own handicapping perspective. When Sam's support staff remove the limitations from their vision, they thereby remove the shackles from Sam's life, allowing him to explore new interests and relationships that will carry him far beyond a life devoted to a coloring book.

Offering Alternatives

Now is when the "right-ist" frequently speaks up and proclaims, in pained disbelief, "Do you mean they should take Sam's coloring book away from him?" The answer is always no. Only a fool would take things away from people. Taking something away from someone is neither an alternative nor a solution.

When people are offered appropriate options, they are more likely to choose those objects and activities that will enhance their acceptance and thus bring them more opportunities for participation and relationships. Unless held back by some external force, most people yearn for the greater range of options and increased freedom of movement of adulthood. It is a natural tendency, common to people all over the world, to "put away childish things." Thus, there is no reason to take away items and events that are not age appropriate, because an adult who has adult opportunities will seldom choose the limitations imposed by childish things. They will more likely choose the increased range of choice making and personal autonomy brought about by participation in age-appropriate activities with age peers. (Note that some of us may choose to collect toys or wear cartoon character T-shirts, but because we have competence, people are not likely to see those things as childish.)

MAXIM: *Only a fool would take things away from people.*

Instead Sam can be offered more alternatives. Then, if he does choose sitting in his room holding his coloring book, it's not because he didn't know that he could also choose going down to the Blue Ribbon on Monday night to watch the game or walking down to the park to pitch horseshoes with other men his age.

Critics may respond that participation in adult activities is unrealistic for a person with severe disabilities. But, only through ridding ourselves of the perceptual blinders that limit our expectations for others and ourselves will we be able to truly facilitate the blessings of Universal Enhancement. It is certainly unrealistic to expect that Sam will become a rocket scientist or president of the United States; but it is definitely not unrealistic to expect him to have the opportunity to have a full, adult life of his choosing.

Professional habilitators are often so bound by systems of goals and plans and training programs that they fail to see the wonderful train-

It's their right

Regardless of sex, sexual orientation, religion, race, national origin, handicapping condition or individual's age, when given options, individuals will choose those options which enhance their dignity and respect.

ing opportunities available through participation in everyday adult activities. Staff may keep Sam from going to the bar to watch the game, because he has to stay home and work on his leisure skills training program. Or they may fail to appreciate that by playing horseshoes with his buddies down the street at the park, Sam will learn social skills–turn-taking, standing in line and eye-hand coordination –while also developing relationships and having fun (an activity which is usually not included in the program plan).

MAXIM: *There is no regulation for having a life.*

Having A Life

- *There are no regulatory requirements for supporting people in getting a life*
- ***When was the last time you were "cited" because persons receiving support:***

Tag 5.30	**were not missed when they were away?**
Tag 3.21	**had no one to send them a birthday card?**
Tag 2.42	**were not taught how to whistle or snap their fingers?**
Tag 5.81	**were not smiling?**
Tag 5.33	**were not told how "handsome" or "attractive" they look when all dressed up to go to church?**
Tag 1.19	**were not encouraged to make a snowman on the day of the first big snow?**
Tag 3.22	**were denied an opportunity for a consensual sexual relationship?**
Tag 9.39	**were not greeted by support staff with a warm "How are you doing today?"**

TALE

The Great Playground Massacre

People who attempt to alter environments in conformance to contemporary standards of age appropriateness are often rejected and scorned, like the prophet who is "without honor in his own country."

When I took a position as assistant superintendent at a large state-run facility, charged with the responsibility of implementing the kinds of principles espoused in Universal Enhancement, I set out to make some changes that were popular neither with the staff nor with the families of the people who lived there.

One obvious problem was that immediately adjacent to a living area occupied only by adults was a child's playground. I would ride past on my way to the administration building and see 43-year-old men sliding down the sliding board and 50-year-old women riding the rocking snail. Sometimes two gray-haired "toddlers" sat together digging holes in the sandbox. Finally, it was too much for me. I felt indignant when I observed people older than me, people who should be experiencing dignity and respect, engaged in childish activities that, to me, seemed demeaning. They had a right to be offered options–options that were more age appropriate.

So I met with a number of the residents of the institution and discussed with them what alternative recreation and relaxation items they might be interested in having on the campus grounds. The residents made many excellent recommendations. I gave the orders, and big changes were made.

The next morning, workmen arrived and removed the sliding boards and the jungle gyms, the merry-go-rounds and the Dumbo swings. In their place, a new park started to take shape. It was a park for adults–park benches, basketball courts, horseshoe pits, curved walks with nice landscaping, porch type glides, outdoor tables and chairs for playing board games or just sipping an al fresco cup of coffee.

The staff was livid. They felt their playground had been destroyed. They convened a meeting of residents and staff and called me before this tribunal to defend my actions.

I listened quietly as one staff person after another made the case that the residents' rights had been violated, that they had lost something precious, that the people who lived in that unit loved those Dumbo swings.

Finally, one of the women who lived at the institution, a frail, elderly woman who was sitting in a wheelchair near the back of the room, raised her hand. She was recognized to speak, and the roomful of people fell silent as they strained to hear her frail voice.

"I think I know why he did it," she said, and stopped for a breath. "He took out the little kids' toys, because... we're not children anymore."

The silence that followed lasted a long time.

I finally found my voice and said, "That's right; you're not children anymore. And now that you're truly adults, you'll never be treated like children again."

No one is likely to offer adult opportunities to children. If we see people with intellectual disabilities or elderly people or people with physical impairments as children, treat them as children, and surround them with the images of childhood, they will likely fulfill our prophecy and act like children. They will not have the opportunity to experience risk, love, autonomy, all the things we looked forward to when, as children, we dreamed of being grown-ups.

R-E-S-P-E-C-T

Respect is another prerogative of adulthood. Unfortunately, children in our society are generally not accorded the same respect and courtesy extended to adults. One could certainly make the case that children, as human beings, are entitled to that respect, but we often couple respect with competence, because in our modern Western culture, we revere competence. We respect people who have proven themselves through their accomplishments, their abilities, their performance. Those among us whose capabilities fall below the normative threshold, usually through no fault of their own, often become the targets of disrespect. It is no prize to be considered childish.

It is likely that people who don't know our friend Sam, seeing the child's coloring book he is carrying, will not offer him the respect usually given a man of his age. Once again, the self-fulfilling prophecy rears its ugly head.

What happens to people who do not receive respect? They don't give it, either. They become Outsiders, and their failure to demonstrate respect justifies their outsider status. They are caught in a vicious cycle. Can anyone be surprised that the woman who is treated like a child is on a training program to reduce tantrums?

Doing "Stupid" Things

Already briefly alluded to is one of the hot human rights issues that are affected by our attitudes toward age appropriateness–alcohol use. Likewise, there is a whole range of health and safety concerns that impose one standard for adults and another for children. Just as we don't let children drink alcohol, we also don't let them use tobacco or engage in sexual intercourse. We don't let them eat too much junk food. We don't let them get involved in relationships we think might be harmful to them.

Similar judgments are made about adult behavior. There are many issues in which most of us believe there is a smart way to act (typically,

RESPECT

Responsive
Encouraging
Sensitive
Perceptive
Expediting
Caring
Thoughtful

It must start with respecting yourself

alcohol in moderation, no tobacco use, a sensible diet, relationships with decent people) and a stupid way to act (drunkenness, chain smoking, compulsive eating, promiscuity). Being responsible caretakers of our own offspring, we feel obligated to keep them from engaging in stupid behavior. The fact that there are no laws prohibiting excessive or unhealthy behavior in adults, though, demonstrates our general societal attitude that adults have the right to do stupid things–unless, that is, the adult has not passed the Gatekeepers' competency test. Outsiders lose the opportunity to make stupid adult choices and, instead, continue to live under the double standard, that supports our making protective decisions for children.

This is not to say that people with disabilities should use alcohol or tobacco, eat themselves into obesity, or enter into abusive relationships (for the same reasons we don't advocate these behaviors for Normatives). Assisting people we support with developing an understanding both of the range of options available and of the consequences that go with each option, will enhance their ability to make reasonably informed decisions themselves. As stated earlier (in a section of Chapter 2), in order to offer an appropriate set of options we have to balance the risk with the opportunity.

When people with disabilities and other Outsiders are treated as children, often we don't even consider some opportunities, and don't even begin to weigh the risks versus the benefits. We may think of that class of opportunities as being available only to adults. Thus we encourage Sam to color in his childish coloring book, but never even consider the possibility of his taking an art class at the local community center.

We decide tobacco use is a health risk and, therefore, Walter (IQ 65) should be weaned off his chewing tobacco. But, we establish policies for where and when staff can smoke in Walter's home.

We decide Sheila (IQ 61) is not ready to go on a date with the man she met at the workshop. But, we rearrange the staff schedule because Yvonne (IQ 98), who was recently hired to work nights, had a rough morning dealing with her abusive husband and didn't show up for work tonight.

We put Joe (IQ 24) on a 1500 calorie diet because he is 10 pounds over his ideal body weight, while Zeke (IQ 117) goes on medical leave for the heart attack brought about by his high cholesterol and high blood pressure.

Once again, the point is that being an adult is determined by age and not by IQ (or any other test of competence). People who are adults should have the opportunities that adults have, including the opportunity to do stupid things, the opportunity to fail.

We heard a story (told by Lynne Seagle of Hope House Foundation in Norfolk, Va.) of a man with intellectual disabilities who had recently moved out of a group home into his own home. (The move highlights the fact that "group home" may be an oxymoron). His mother had left him a small trust fund when she died, and it was this money that he used, supervised by his aunt, to maintain the house in which he lived. One day, the staff who supported him could not find him and discovered that his trust fund money was missing, too. A week later, he returned, broke. He had run off with a stripper he had met in a bar, and she had helped him spend his savings before she disappeared. The agency staff were upset with him for having been so irresponsible. His reply was, "It was the best date I ever had."

Now, who are we to say that that man should not have had the opportunity to blow his savings on the best date he ever had? Would we want someone breathing down our necks, constantly monitoring to make sure we always made smart decisions? Of course not. Why should it be any different for people with disabilities?

TALE

You and I

by Elaine Popovich

Lutheran School Services

I am a resident. You reside.

I am admitted. You move in.

I have behavior problems. You are rude.

I am non-compliant. You don't like being told what to do.

When I ask you out to dinner, it is an outing. When you ask someone out, it is a date.

I don't know how many people have read the progress notes people write about me. I don't even know what's in there. You didn't speak to your best friend for a month after she read your journal.

I make mistakes during my check-writing program. Someday I might get a bank account. You forget to record some withdrawals from your account. The bank calls to remind you.

I wanted to talk with the nice looking person behind us at the grocery store. I was told that it was inappropriate to talk to strangers. You met your spouse in the produce department. He couldn't find the bean sprouts.

I celebrated my birthday yesterday with five other residents and two staff members. I hope my family sends a card. Your family threw you a surprise party. You brother couldn't make it from out of state. It sounded wonderful.

My case manager sends a report every month to my guardian. It says everything I did wrong and some things I did right. You are still mad at your sister for calling your mom after you got a speeding ticket.

I am on a special diet because I am five pounds over my ideal weight. Your doctor gave up telling you.

I am learning household skills. You hate housework.

I am learning leisure skills. Your shirt says you are a "couch potato."

After I do my budget program tonight, I might get to go to McDonald's if I have enough money. You were glad the new French restaurant took your charge card.

My case manager, psychologist, R.N., occupational therapist, physical therapist, nutritionist and house staff set goals for me for next year. You haven't decided what you want out of life.

Someday I will be discharged… maybe. You will move onward and upward.

It is important to be mindful of the special obligations and responsibilities taken on by agencies that operate under contractual oversight demands (See Volume Two, Chapter 2). The challenge faced by such organizations is to offer and encourage bounded options–neither supporting the anything goes attitude of total license, nor succumbing to the nothing doing stance of the institution. From an organizational and professional perspective we have a covenant with those we support: do no harm.

A great deal of space has been devoted to the issue of age appropriateness because it is crucial to the final step in Universal Enhancement, inclusion in the community. If we see people with competence limitations as children, in the interest of keeping them safe, we will not allow them the opportunities to take risks, to explore the world in which they live. We will continue to keep them sheltered away from the community and will not allow them to become participants of the communities in which they live. They will not be afforded the same opportunities we cherish and demand as adults, and they will never be able to live full lives, lives replete with both success and failure, with smart decisions as well as stupid ones.

No one told us we had to be perfect in order to be treated as adults. Let's not hold a double standard for people who have failed some kind of test of acceptance.

TALE

Trick or Treat

I was conducting a presentation one early October for an agency that provided residential and habilitation services to people with disabilities.

While I was talking about age appropriateness, I noticed an older woman in the audience who seemed extremely distressed. Having occasionally listened to parents argue the case for continuing to treat their adult offspring as children, I assumed I knew why the woman was upset. Perhaps she thought I was advocating taking an age inappropriate item away from her son or daughter, something the mother felt was necessary to show that she cared for her "handicapped child."

When it was time for a break, the woman remained in her seat, apparently deep in thought. I asked one of my hosts who she was.

The man replied, "Oh, she's a member of our board of directors, and she has a son who has Down syndrome."

"How old is her son?" I asked.

"I think he's about 35," the host replied. "He attends our sheltered workshop."

This information bore out my initial appraisal. Just as I was about to head for the refreshment table, the woman approached me, a deep frown furrowing her brow, the trace of a tear on her cheek.

"Dr. Pomeranz," she said, "can I speak with you a minute?"

Here it comes, I thought: "I love my child. He's my baby, and he'll always be my baby. Why can't he sit on the floor and play with his rubber ducky? He needs to be protected." It was the all too frequently heard parental objection to treating adults as adults.

"Sure," I said. "What's on your mind?"

"Well," said the woman, pausing for breath, "I've been thinking about what you were saying, and I've come to a decision. I'd like to share it with you." She paused again to compose her words.

"You know that Halloween is coming up. Well, my decision is that this will be the first time in 30 years that I'm not going to dress my son up in a clown costume and parade him up and down the street trick-or-treating." Her voice broke a little. I could see that this was a difficult and significant moment for her.

"What do you think your son would like to do instead?" I asked.

"I think," she replied, "he'd like to stay home and help pass out the candy to the kids who come to the door."

Toolbox

Making the Use of Time Meaningful

Sometimes it's a real challenge to identify training and leisure items that are appropriate to a person's age but which are not too challenging to his or her degree of competence. We have to be creative to meet that challenge. Items need not be utilized in the way they are intended, in order for a person to enjoy interacting with them. Here are some ideas:

PUZZLES: Adults play with puzzles, but the typical 500-piece jigsaw puzzle is too difficult for some people. The alternative 10-piece puzzle is usually a picture of Barney or Rainbow Brite or some other subject that is suitable for 5-year-olds but not for 50-year-olds.

A simple solution is to make your own puzzle. Just assist the person in selecting and purchasing a vinyl place mat with the typical landscape scene of boats in a harbor or autumn leaves or ocean waves–scenes, that interest the puzzle-maker. Turn the place mat so the picture is face down, and divide it into six segments (or fewer, depending on the individual's ability) with a felt-tipped pen. Cut along the lines, turn the pieces back over and voila!–a six-piece puzzle. If the puzzle master gets good at this one, cut the pieces in half–a 12-piece puzzle!

COLORING BOOKS: Many adults like to draw and paint. If we support someone who has this desire but has limited competence, we tend to buy coloring books and crayons. Most coloring books, though, are made for little children. They have clowns and puppy dogs and cartoon characters as subject matter. And most adults haven't used wax crayons in years.

Instead of a coloring book and crayons, help the person you're supporting to purchase a tablet of blank drawing paper and a package of multi-colored felt-tipped markers or colored pencils. Now the person has an "artist's pad" and can indulge his or her penchant for graphic expression.

GAMES: Many adult board games require reading skills and the ability to develop complex strategies. But some don't.

UNO® is a card game often played by groups of people that include people who have disabilities. It's fun, fast, and simple. If you can match colors, you can play.

Bingo is another easy board game played by adults. Try to avoid "picture" Bingo. The pictures are usually very childish.

Jenga® (also known as Ta-Ka-Ra-Di) is a game of stacking small blocks. It helps develop strategic thinking and fine motor skills–and not a cartoon figure in sight!

When buying items, don't worry about their intended use. Many puzzles that are designed to test complex problem-solving skills (and are very challenging on that level) may also be used simply as interesting things to manipulate. Many adult hours of interest and attention can be focused on such things as:

- Rubic's Cube
- Hourglasses
- Eight-ball fortune teller
- Sliding numbers puzzle
- Brain teasers
- Magnetic cut-outs.

These are just a few ideas. You and the people you support will probably have many other ideas once given the opportunity to experience a variety of media.

The trick is: Don't take something away; replace it with something appropriate to the person's age. Give options!

About the Author

Thomas E. Pomeranz, Ed.D. is a nationally recognized authority, clinician and consultant in the field of developmental disabilities. Over the last 30 years, Dr. Pomeranz has conducted hundreds of seminars and programs throughout the United States and Canada. He was the keynote presenter at the Fifth International Conference on Developmental Disabilities and Aging in Cyprus, Greece. Additionally, Dr. Pomeranz is noted for his innovative approach to leadership and management training.

Dr. Pomeranz holds bachelor and master of science degrees in education and mental retardation from Indiana University, and has done post-graduate work in experimental psychology at Notre Dame University. He received his doctorate from Indiana University with a concentration in mental health administration. Dr. Pomeranz has held top-level positions in three large state-operated facilities as well as community-based service organizations. Throughout his career, Dr. Pomeranz has held faculty posts in several universities and is currently an adjunct faculty member of Saint Louis University's School of Public Health.

Dr. Pomeranz is the principal consultant of ResCare Training Technologies, the external training and consulting business of ResCare, the nation's largest provider of services for people with developmental disabilities.

A Note on the Type

The text of this book was set in Electra, a typeface designed in 1935 by the renowned designer and illustrator William A. Dwiggins (1880-1956). A standard book typeface since its release due to the evenness of design and high legibility, this face cannot be classified as either modern or old style. It is not based on any historical model, nor does it echo any particular period or style. It avoids the extreme contrasts between thick and thin elements that mark most modern faces, and it gives a feeling of fluidity, warmth, personality, and speed.

Printed and bound by McNaughton & Gunn Inc.,
Saline, Michigan

Cover illustration by Barton Stabler
Cover and book design by Diane J. Bell
The artwork in this book is a compilation of clip art and original drawings.
The original drawings are by various artists, none of whom expect to receive credit, except where indicated in the image.